ENGINEER YOUR ACCENT

How to Speak English with an American Accent in Less Than 10 Weeks

Rebecca Zhuo and
Peter Kowalke

© 2019 Engineer Your Accent

Rebecca Zhuo and Peter Kowalke

Engineer Your Accent: How to Speak English with
an American Accent in Less Than 10 Weeks

SECOND EDITION

All rights reserved. No part of this publication may be
reproduced, stored in a retrieval system or transmitted
in any form or by any means, electronic, mechanical,
photocopying, recording or otherwise without the prior
permission of the authors or in accordance with the
provisions of the Copyright, Designs and Patents Act 1988
or under the terms of any license permitting limited
copying issued by the Copyright Licensing Agency.

*To engineers around the world: thank you
for creating the future, for believing that
something new and better can exist.*

*This book is for you. To empower you to be able to
connect and to collaborate across languages and
cultures in service of creating a better tomorrow.*

CONTENTS

Title Page	1
Copyright	2
Dedication	3
How I Became an Accent Engineer	7
Learn Sounds, Not Words	13
Remap the Sound Variants	15
Engineer Consonant Sounds	19
Engineer Vowel Sounds	25
Accent Engineering in Practice	29
Join Our Team	40
About the Authors	43

HOW I BECAME AN ACCENT ENGINEER

Hi.

I'm Rebecca, founder of Engineer Your Accent.

I want to congratulate you on saying yes to yourself and taking this huge step toward learning a new accent.

Working on your accent helps people understand you better, and this can up-level your career, your relationships, and your life in general. Having a native accent can make a big difference if you live and work in a foreign country, or even if you're just talking with someone in another country via a conference call.

Being understood is a powerful thing. Even more importantly, though, speaking with a native accent helps you communicate confidently. When you know you are pronouncing words the "correct" way, you reduce your self-consciousness. You empower yourself.

Since this empowerment aspect is why I started Engineer Your Accent, let me tell you how it all began.

It All Started With My Team

I love empowering people. That's why I'm a project manager in Silicon Valley. I manage deliverables and juggle logistics, but my real job as a project manager is empowering my team so they can do their best work.

With one of my teams, we had a large, diverse group that hailed from all over the world. Everyone on the project was excited, working together and contributing to our goal. It was great, and good things were happening.

But there also was a problem, one that really caught me off guard.

I noticed that although the team was great on Slack,

interacting and talking freely, this wasn't the case when they came together in person. In person, my team didn't have the interactions and idea-sharing that I was used to seeing from them online.

The native English speakers were the same in person, but the Indians, Chinese and other non-native speakers weren't themselves. They weren't talking as much, they weren't contributing in the same way.

This was an issue, and I began asking myself what was going on.

Self-consciousness about accents was going on, I came to realize.

This wasn't a language problem. Everyone on my team knew English. Sure, sometimes there would be a word or phrase that wasn't quite right. But this problem wasn't about language—we were fine on Slack, and verbally it was no different.

What was different was that the non-native speakers felt there was a problem. They were self-conscious about their accent. Even though the native English speakers didn't notice or care, the accent issue mattered a lot to the non-native speakers.

This kept the non-native speakers from speaking

up as much in person, and it made them lose confidence whenever they would talk with a native speaker face-to-face.

That bothered me. A lot. I wanted to help my team succeed.

Accents are Easy—We're Going About it All Wrong

Fortunately, I studied physics and linguistics in college before becoming a project manager. So I took a first-principles approach and felt empowered enough to actually ask the questions: Why do we have accents, and why do we often spend decades in a country and still talk with an accent even though we know the language?

When I looked at the problem of accents from a first-principles perspective, I discovered that it isn't actually that hard to learn a new accent. Most people are just going about it all wrong

That's because what's really going on with accents is a simple mapping problem.

There's a finite number of sounds that humans can make, I knew from my linguistics training. But each language only uses a subset of these sounds. So each of us grows up learning some sounds and ignoring others.

The problem is when we learn a new language that uses a different subset of sounds, some of which we don't know. So our brain ingeniously maps the missing sound to the closest sound it already knows, the best it can do.
That's why someone who knows English can still talk with an accent even 30 years after learning the language. They know the language—they're just not making the right sounds because they have it mapped wrongly in their head.

Adjusting Our Accent is Easy—We've Got This One

I'll admit, I got really excited when I looked at this problem and realized it was just a mapping issue.

That's because there's only a few sounds that are different between languages; you can adjust your accent by learning just a few new sounds.

Engineering a new accent isn't actually that hard! You can spend 10 years with an accent and never make any progress because you're using the same sounds you've always used, or you can identify the few sounds that are different, make a few adjustments, and begin speaking like a native speaker in as little as 10 weeks.

I got even more excited when I tried this approach with some of my teammates. It worked like a charm!

It worked so well, in fact, that those I helped began getting mistaken for native speakers; people from their own country would come up to them and ask where they grew up. These people thought that my team members grew up in the U.S., not in their native country! Wow.

This is when I knew I was onto something. This was when Engineer Your Accent was born.

Accents are wonderful; I love hearing the diversity of accents in the Silicon Valley. But if someone feels disempowered because of their accent, if they feel shy or lose their voice because they are self-conscious about their accent, I don't like that. That's when accents are not good, and when it is time to engineer your accent so you speak like a native speaker.

This book is all about empowering you and showing you how.

LEARN SOUNDS, NOT WORDS

Engineering your accent is easy. You just need the right framework.

The traditional view is that improving an accent is hard. If you want to sound like a native speaker, the thinking goes, you must grow up around the language or work on it actively for years. Sometimes it even takes a lifetime of practice before you get rid of your accent.

But this is not true. Improving your accent it easy. Most people just tackle the problem in the wrong way.

The framework that most people use for improving their accent is addressing the problem at the word level. This means learning the right way to say each word. The problem with this approach is that nobody can learn the right way to say every word. There are just too many words. So while many people learn a new language, most retain some of the pronunciation habits of their native tongue because they memorize the sound of particular words instead of learning the fundamental sounds of the new language.

A better framework, the one we will use, is learning the sounds of the new language. These are the building blocks that will help you automatically pronounce words the way a native speaker might. This is a first-principles approach to accent improvement, and it makes the process really simple and fast.

There are thousands of words in a given language, sometimes even millions. But there are only a few sounds. In the English language, for instance, there are roughly 1,022,000 words, with several thousand new ones added each year. But there are only 44 sounds in the English language. That's not many!

If you master this small number of sounds for a given language, you will be able to speak like a native speaker in no time.

REMAP THE SOUND VARIANTS

Accents come from sounds in the new language that don't exist in your native tongue. When you encounter a sound that you don't have in your native language, your brain picks the closest sound it does know.

So forget having to learn all the sounds of a new language. You just have to focus on the few sounds that are missing from the language you grew up with as a child.

Let me explain.

In chemistry, we have the Periodic Table of Elements. The elements on that list are the building blocks used for building everything else. They are fundamental.

In linguistics, the scientific study of the world's languages, we have something similar: the International Phonetic Alphabet. The building blocks for this international phonetic alphabet are sounds, and the list of sounds on this phonetic alphabet includes all the sounds that humans are capable of producing as a species.

Now when you're a baby, you have access to all the sounds that humans are capable of producing; you have the whole phonetic alphabet. You play with these sounds and just have fun with them. You babble.

But as you get older—and we're talking about days here, not years—you start listening to the sounds around you and comparing them to the sounds you're making when you babble. You play the game of trying to reproduce these sounds you're hearing.

You play this game over, and over, and over again as a baby and a child, making the same sounds as the people around you until you get them just right. These sounds become the ones you know and master, because they're the ones that are used every day. These are the sounds that people use when they speak, and the sounds that you use when you learn to speak.

Each language in the world is just a subset of the phonetic alphabet, however. Your mother tongue only uses some of the possible sounds that humans can make.

So if you grew up in India, you might have the Hindi subset of sounds. And if you grew up in the United States, you have the American English subset of sounds.

These subsets are not the same, so they overlap but they don't overlap completely.

So what happens when you grow up in India and then learn American English, for instance, is that you start with the wrong subset of sounds. You're missing some of the sounds you need.

Your brain is pretty crafty, though. When it encounters a sound that it doesn't know, it maps the new sound to the closest sound that it does know.

This mapping of new sounds to the closest equivalent in your native tongue is so predictable, we can actually define what constitutes an Indian accent or a Chinese accent; we know an accent right away because the mapping is so consistent across speakers.

So this is what's really going on when someone has an accent. That's why people still have their accent even after 30 years of living in a country, too. They learn new words, they master the grammar, they speak the language for decades. But they never change their sound mapping. So they still have their accent; they're still using an incomplete sound subset and sounding like a foreigner when they talk instead of sounding like a native.

Let's not fall into that trap. Let's work on these missing sounds and add them to your sound repertoire so you are mapping sounds correctly for the new language.

We don't need to learn every word of a language to eliminate our accent. We don't even need to learn every sound in a language. All we need is the remapping of a few variant sounds that exist in the new language but are not in our native tongue.

ENGINEER CONSONANT SOUNDS

L et's start talking about sounds.

There are actually only three variables that control what a sound "sounds" like. For consonants there are three variables, and for vowels there are three different variables.

When you understand these variables, you can easily engineer your accent by making sound adjustments so you produce the correct sound for a language instead of the variant sound that gives you an accent.

We'll work on consonant sound mechanics in this chapter, and we'll cover vowel mechanics in the next.

As I mentioned, there are only three variables that control for all the consonant sounds humans are capable of producing. These variables are:

1. Place of articulation (where the tongue goes).

2. Manner of articulation (what the air does while vocalizing the sound).

3. Voiced or unvoiced (whether the vocal cords vibrate or not).

Let's look at each of these variables one at a time.

Place of Articulation: Where the Tongue Goes

The first variable is the place of articulation. This is the placement of your tongue when you make a consonant sound.

For example, is the sound made with just your tongue, or with your lips, too? Is your tongue between your teeth, with your tongue touching the teeth? Maybe your tongue is a little farther back in the mouth where that ridge is at the top of your mouth.

The image below illustrates some of the places of articulation, the places where a consonant sound can occur.

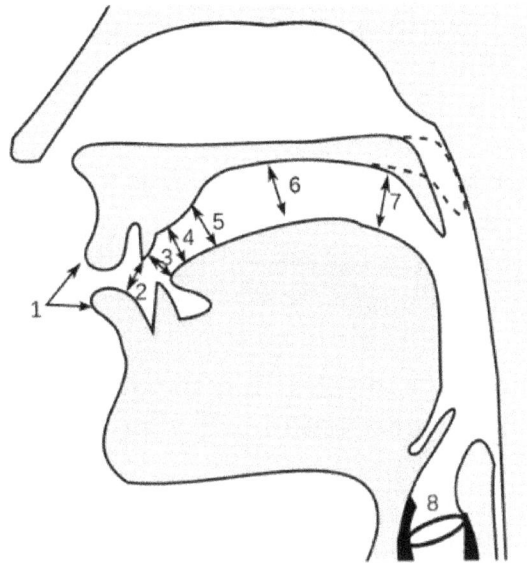

Place Of Articulation by Tavin (CC BY 3.0)

Manner of Articulation: What the Air Does

Next we have the manner of articulation. When we

make a sound, what's the airflow like?

For instance, when we make a sound, the air might get caught in the mouth and then explode out like it does with an American English *P* sound.

Make a *P* sound right now, and you'll notice a little puff of air as you vocalize the sound. If you pay attention, you can feel the air get caught, stop, and then explode out of the mouth.

There are other things your mouth can do with airflow, too. Maybe the air is flowing through a very narrow constriction in the mouth like when your tongue is between your teeth and you're making the American *TH* sound.

When you make the *TH* sound, the air flows through that narrow constriction and almost cools your tongue.

Or, maybe your tongue never touches any part of your mouth, and there's a lot of room for the air to flow through easily.

These are all possible manners of articulation for a sound.

  1. Nasal: Air flows through the nose and mouth.

  2. Stop: Air gets caught in a stop, then explodes

out.

3. Fricative: Air is forced through a narrow constriction in the mouth.

4. Affricate: Air gets caught in a stop, then is forced through a narrow constriction in the mouth.

5. Approximant: Air flows freely; some constriction at the place of articulation (see above), but not enough to create much turbulence.

Voiced or Unvoiced: If the Vocal Cords Vibrate

There's a third variable for consonants, too. Do the vocal cords vibrate?

This is a binary variable. Either they vibrate, which we call a "voiced" sound. Or they don't vibrate, which we call "unvoiced."

You can tell if a sound is voiced or unvoiced by putting your finger at the base of your throat when you speak.

Say "Hello world."

If you put your finger on your throat when you say it, you feel your vocal cords vibrate. There are some voiced sounds in that sentence!

Another good example is the difference between the American S and Z sounds. The variables for these two sounds are exactly the same except S is unvoiced and Z is voiced. If you make the S sound, your vocal cords will not vibrate. But if you vibrate your vocal cords during pronunciation, you get the Z sound.

Some languages have voiced consonants, such as American English. Others do not; the Chinese languages completely lack this consonant sound feature.

If your native language lacks a sound feature, that's not a problem; you just need to learn its mechanics. You could make these sounds when you were a baby, and you can easily learn them again.

ENGINEER VOWEL SOUNDS

Now that you understand how consonant sounds work, let's explore the mechanics of vowel sounds. Once you understand the mechanics of vowel sounds, you will have all you need for engineering a new accent and sounding like a native speaker.

With consonants, we have three variables that come together to create those sounds. Those variables are place of articulation (where the tongue goes), manner of articulation (what the air does while vocalizing the sound), and whether the sound is voiced or unvoiced (whether the vocal cords vibrate or not).

Vowel sounds are different, though. That's why they are vowels, a different sound category.

For vowels, the manner of articulation is fixed. It always has no constriction; air just flows through the mouth with no constriction. So that variable is out.

Vocal cords always vibrate for vowels, too. So that variable drops out as well. Chinese native speakers do not have voiced consonants, for instance, but they do have voiced vowels because all vowels are voiced. So when we explain the voiced mechanic to a Chinese native speaker, we have to relate it to vowel sounds.

This just leaves us with the place of articulation: Where the tongue goes. So the only thing we're playing with inside the mouth is the placement of the tongue. We break this into two separate variables, x-axis and y-axis, because that makes it easier.

Two is not quite enough variables, though, so vowels also have an additional mechanic that is unique to vowels: the shape of the mouth when making the sound.

So there are three variables for vowels, but they are different variables than the ones we need for consonants.

Let's look at each of these variables one at a time.

Place of Articulation (Vertical): Height of the Tongue

The first variable is how high or low the tongue is in the mouth. The tongue can be high, middle or low.

If you move your tongue up toward the roof of your mouth, you're high. If you hide your tongue in the bottom of your mouth, you're at the middle. If the mouth opens wide and the tongue burrows into the bottom of the mouth, that's the low position.

Place of Articulation (Horizontal): Depth of the Tongue

Your tongue can move forward or backward, too. That's the depth of your tongue when making a vowel sound. The three positions for this variable are front, center, and pulled back into the mouth.

Good examples of this horizontal movement are the American *E* (as in "beat") and *OO* (as in "boot") sounds. If you make the *E* sound in American English, your tongue is forward in your mouth, near your teeth. But if you make the *OO* sound, your tongue slides back into your mouth (and downward to the floor; can you guess the vertical position with this sound?)

Roundedness: What the Lips Do

Finally, the third variable for making vowel sounds is what the lips do, which affects the roundedness of the vowel. Are the lips pursed like you're kissing someone? Are they pulled back in a smile when you make the sound? Is the mouth open like you're surprised?

For the American *E* sound, for instance, your face is in a smile when you make the sound correctly. But when you sound out the *OO* sound, your lips are round like you're puckering up for a kiss.

So there you have it. Those are your boundary and reference points for vowels, the variables you work with when engineering a vowel sound. You now have all that you need for engineering an accent.

In the next chapter, we'll show you how to put it all together and start engineering your accent for a given language.

ACCENT ENGINEERING IN PRACTICE

Now that you have the theory and a greater understanding of how sounds are produced, you can successfully engineer your accent with a little practice.

The key is finding the sounds in the new language that don't exist in your native tongue, then practicing those sounds until you build the muscle memory.

With practice, you can expand the range of sounds available to you and automatically use the right sounds for the language you are speaking in. This is how you engineer your accent for a new language in less than 10 weeks. One motivated client of ours even mastered an American accent in less than two hours (although that was unusually fast).

The Engineer Your Accent Game Plan

We recommend five steps for successfully engineering a new accent, a slightly modified version of the same steps we use for our online course.

Step 1: Define the Sound Variance

What are the sounds in the new language that do not map properly to the sounds in your native tongue? These are the sounds you need for your new language that do not exist in your native language, the sounds that are mapped improperly and creating your accent.

Start by identifying the sound inventory for your native language; those are the sounds you grew up with in your hometown. You'll find this sound inventory by doing a quick search online for the International Phonetic Alphabet (IPA) for your native language.

If you are Indian, for instance, you might search for

"international phonetic alphabet hindi" and arrive at the Wikipedia page that lists all the IPA sounds for Hindi and Urdu. You'll get something like this:

IPA[1]	Hindi[1]	ISO 15919 [1]	Urdu	Approximate English equivalent
b	ब	ba	ب	butter
bʰ	भ	bha	بھ	abhor
d[2]	द	da	د	the
dʰ[2]	ध	dha	دھ	within (as a *dhh* sound, tongue touches palate, strong air exhalation)

Next, find the sound inventory for your new language.

Here are the sound inventories for the American English consonants and vowels to help you get started:

American English Consonants:

				PLACE OF ARTICULATION				
MANNER OF ARTICULATION		BILABIAL	LABIO DENTAL	INTER DENTAL	ALVEOLAR	ALVEO- PALATAL	PALATAL	VELAR	GLOTTAL
	NASAL	m			n			ŋ	
	STOP	p b			t d			k g	
	FRICATIVE		f v	θ ð	s z	ʃ ʒ			h
	AFFRICATE					tʃ dʒ			
	LATERAL APPROXIMANT				l				
	RETROFLEX APPROXIMANT				ɹ				
	GLIDE	w					j		

* Sounds on the left side of each box are pronounced without vibrating the vocal cords. Sounds on the

right side of each box are pronounced while vibrating the vocal cords.

American English Vowels:

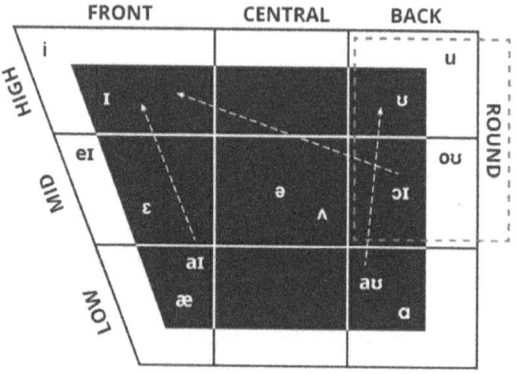

* Sounds on the inside black portion of the vowel chart are tense vowels. Sounds on the outer white portion are lax vowels.

Now that you have the sound inventory for both your native language and your new language, go through your new language and figure out which IPA sounds are not in your native language. You can do this by comparing the IPA letter for each sound in your new language and seeing if you have that same IPA letter in your native language.

If Hindi is your native language and American English is your new language, for instance, you will discover that both Hindi and American English have the same IPA letter for the *NG* sound, ŋ. That means you won't have an accent when producing the American English *NG* sound. But if you look at the two charts, you also will find that Hindi does not have the IPA letter for the American *T* sound. This means you will have an accent when you sound out the American *T* sound.

Take note of the sounds in your new language that don't exist in your native language. This is the sound variance, and this is what you'll need to work on.

Step 2: Engineer the Sound Adjustment

Now that you know the sounds you will need to learn (or re-learn, since you had access to all the sounds when you were a baby), the next step is picking one of those sounds in the sound variance and engineering the adjustments you need to make for pronouncing the sound correctly.

There are four parts to this process for a given sound.

2.1. Find the Technical Explanation for Producing the Sound

Search online for the technical explanation of how

the IPA sound is produced by a human mouth. This technical explanation should show you where to place your tongue, what the air is doing when you make the sound, etc.

This explanation defines the correct way to make the sound.

2.2. Define the Variables for the Sound

Each sound has a limited number of variables, as we showed in chapters four and five.

Take the technical explanation for the sound you need to learn, and then define the variables for that given sound.

If your sound is a consonant, where is the tongue located for that sound? What is the air flow supposed to do? Do your vocal cords vibrate? You can review the consonant variables by reviewing chapter four.

If your sound is a vowel, what is the vertical and horizontal placement of your tongue for the sound, and are the lips rounded or not? Chapter five covers the variables for vowels, so you might want to review that chapter as you define the variables for a vowel sound.

2.3. Locate the Closest Sound in Your Native Language

Now that you have defined the variables for the given sound, look for the closest equivalent in your native language, the sound that has the most variables similar to the new sound you want to make.

This likely will come naturally, because your brain already has mapped this sound to the sound in your new language. Our brain is smart like that. But check and see if the existing sound you are making for the new sound is in fact the closest sound from a technical perspective. Do the variables mostly line up?

2.4. Make the Variable Adjustments

Now for the fun, the accent engineering part!

Take the sound in your native language that is close to the new sound and determine the variable adjustments you should make to go from the native sound to the new sound.

For an Indian who is learning the American English T sound, for instance, the lone variable that needs adjustment is the position of the tongue; an Indian

T sound has a curled tongue, and an American English T sound has a flat tongue.

So if you're engineering the American English T sound, all you must do is uncurl your tongue. That's it! All the other variables stay the same.

For most sounds, all you need is one or two adjustments; making new sounds really isn't that hard when you take a first-principles approach!

In many cases, you can make these adjustments even easier by finding a sound in your native language that has the same variable you must adjust. If you must adjust the placement of your tongue so it doesn't curl, for instance, find another sound in your native language that has an uncurled tongue.

Optional Step: Record a Native Speaker Pronouncing the Sound

Once you know the sounds you need, and know the technical adjustments, ask a native speaker if they can pronounce the sound for you, both as a sound and contained within words. Have them repeat the sound and the words several times, and record it with your phone or an audio recorder for later review.

The point is hearing the new sound so you can

mimic it just like you did when you were a baby.

Step 3: Try Your New Sound (and Get Feedback)

Now that you have an understanding of the sounds you need to learn, and the mechanics of how it is made, the all-important third step is trying out your new sound.

Practice making this new sound, paying close attention to each variable while you make the sound. Focus is important with this step so you position your mouth properly for the new sound. You don't yet have muscle memory for the sound, so you need concentration much like you do if you're learning to play a piano.

It also can help if you get live feedback from a native speaker as you practice the sound. This way, you know when you get the sound right. You might not hear the difference if you make a new sound and have the variables slightly off, but a native speaker will know right away because they have heard the correct sound millions of times in the past and know immediately when something sounds wrong.

Step 4: Practice Until There is Muscle

Memory

Deliberately practice the sound you are learning for 5 minutes each day. You don't need hours of practice because your subconscious will do most of the work while you are sleeping; all you need is a few minutes each day so you can build the muscle memory for your new sound.

Like we noted in Step 3, though, you must focus when practicing your new sound. Pay attention to what your mouth is doing when you vocalize the sound, what your tongue is doing, and how your mouth feels overall when you make the sound. Also pay attention to airflow and pressure changes.

Repeat the sound many times, then stop and rest for a bit so your subconscious can integrate what you just practiced. Repeat the exercise again after the rest.

When you automatically make the correct sound during normal conversation, you know you've built the habit for this sound. Congratulations!

Step 5: Repeat for Each New Sound

Learn each variant sound in turn. Don't work on them all at once. Instead, pick a sound and go through steps 2 through 4 until you've mastered the sound and built the muscle memory. Then repeat the process for the next sound you need.

These are the steps we use when helping someone learn a new accent, and we're constantly surprised how fast people pick up these new sounds.

If you practice every day, you can engineer your accent and sound like a native speaker in less than 10 weeks.

Feel Overwhelmed?

Engineering your accent isn't hard. You've got this one. But if you need help, we can walk you through each step in the process and help you overcome that feeling of overwhelm.

You can do this on your own. You really can. But if you feel overwhelmed or want a helping hand, we'd love to help.

Contact us for assistance beyond what is included in this book by emailing **Rebecca@EngineerYourAccent.com**

JOIN OUR TEAM

So many people feel disempowered because of their accent. Maybe you are one of them.

But as you've seen, engineering your accent is not hard. It is a lot easier than most people think! You just have to remap a few sounds, and you can change your accent almost immediately. It doesn't take years of learning how to pronounce thousands of words, it just takes a few new sounds.

Empowering you is why Engineer Your Accent exists, both this book and the course we offer. But we don't just want to empower you, we also would like to help everyone who lacks self-confidence and gets shy when speaking in another language.

So here's the ask.

Will You Help Us Empower Others?

If you're as excited about accent engineering as we are, we'd love your help in spreading the word and empower as many people as possible with their accent.

There are two ways you can join our accent engineering team.

1. Share This Book

Most people struggle with their accent because they don't know there is a better way. That's what this book is all about.

So if you have friends and colleagues who also speak with an accent and want to change that, let them know about accent engineering!

Here's a link you can give others so they can download a sample of this book for free.

EngineerYourAccent.com

2. Join Our Accent Engineers Community

The second way you can join our team is even more exciting. That's because we get to know you directly and have you actively in our community.

Because accent engineering is something we can all do, and something we can help each other with, we're creating an online community where you can connect with others who also are working on their accent. In the community you can help others with their accent engineering, get help yourself, and play a more active role in our mission of empowering people through accent adjustment.

Participating in our Accent Engineers community is a great way to get involved and get extra help with your own journey, too.

You can learn more here:

EngineerYourAccent.com

So will you join us? We'd love to have you on our team.

ABOUT THE AUTHORS

R ebecca Zhuo is a linguist and physicist who applies first-principles thinking to everything. She grew up in the Silicon Valley and is the founder of Engineer Your Accent.

In addition to teaching people how to efficiently learn to speak English with an American accent, Rebecca also builds teams for crowdsourced engineering projects.

For more on Rebecca, visit rebeccazhuo.com

Peter Kowalke is a journalist and author who grew up in Cleveland, Ohio and has spent the past 15 years living in various locations around the world. Every day he interacts with people who speak with an accent.

In addition being a prolific writer, Peter also is a growth and relationship coach who works with clients around the world on personal and relationship empowerment.

More on Peter can be found at peterkowalke.com

www.ingramcontent.com/pod-product-compliance
Lightning Source LLC
Chambersburg PA
CBHW022122090426
42743CB00008B/967